# LONDON 2000+

Chris,

Happy Birthday!

Enjoy London...

# SAM LUBELL

FOREWORD BY KEN LIVINGSTONE

THE MONACELLI PRESS

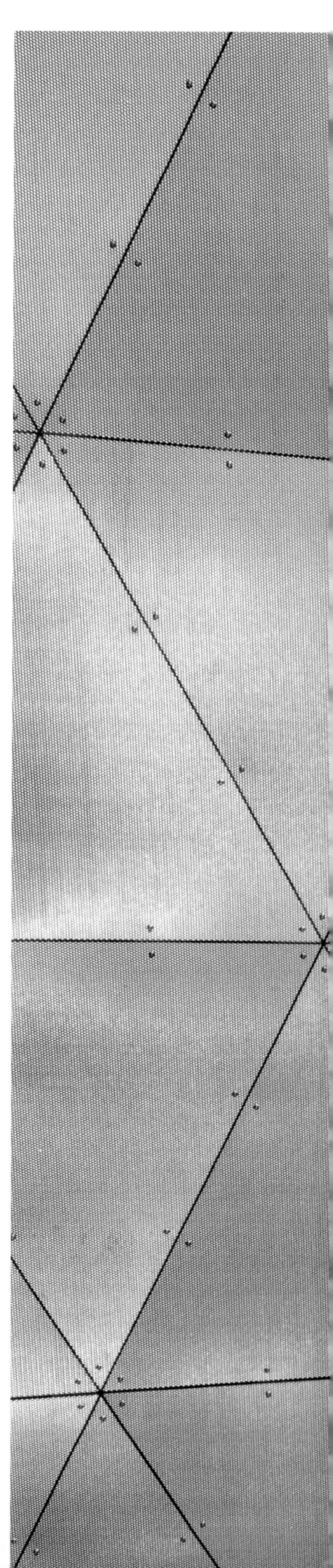

NEW ARCHITECTURE
LONDON
2000+

Thanks to Andrea Monfried and Stacee Lawrence for having faith in me and for putting so much into this project; to Gianfranco Monacelli and Elizabeth White for making the book tangible; to David Blankenship for once again creating a beautiful piece of art; and to my family and Carri for inspiring me every day.

Published in the United States by The Monacelli Press, a division of Random House, Inc., New York.

The Monacelli Press and colophon are trademarks of Random House, Inc.

LIBRARY OF CONGRESS CATALOGING-IN-PUBLICATION DATA
Lubell, Sam.
*London 2000+ : new architecture* / Sam Lubell.
p. cm.
ISBN 978-1-58093-208-0 (hardcover)
1. Architecture — England — London — 21st century.
2. London (England) — Buildings, structures, etc.
I. Title. II. Title: London 2000 plus.
NA970.L83 2008
720.9421'090511 — dc22
2008013223

Printed in China

10 9 8 7 6 5 4 3 2 1

First edition

Text set in Section and Proforma

Designed by David Blankenship

www.monacellipress.com

# FOREWORD
# KEN LIVINGSTONE

MAYOR OF LONDON 2000–2008

**LONDON IS A UNIQUE CITY,** with buildings and districts as diverse as its people. It has always been an open city — open to ideas and to individuals — a city of trade and exchange that looks outward to the world. It is not a formally planned city and indeed its inhabitants, rather than an imposed higher authority, have shaped its distinctive character over many centuries.

Foster + Partners, City Hall, 2002

During its tenure from 2000 to 2008, my administration challenged developers, architects, and planners to come forward with designs for buildings that met tough environmental criteria, respected London's built heritage, and took public transport hubs into consideration. Equally, we made clear that badly designed and poorly constructed buildings are not socially, economically, or environmentally sustainable: they split communities, fail to attract business, and blight both local landscapes and the global environment: we cannot continue to repeat mistakes of the past — too much of our great city has been carelessly developed.

Today, our city is seeing the dramatic transformation intended. In conjunction with Richard Rogers, my advisor on architecture, and Design for London, the city's architecture and urbanism unit, we worked to put responsible new architecture back into the heart of London. Rogers spearheaded the move towards this urban renaissance, and through his leadership we inspired architects, developers, and the public sector to significantly raise standards for all new buildings for a prosperous, better connected, and more environmentally responsible city that offers a better quality of life for Londoners and visitors.

Some of the most exciting new architecture in the world has sealed London's reputation as a truly global city; we hope it will be seen as the city that propelled tall buildings into the twenty-first century: Foster + Partners tore up the rule-book in designing the Swiss Re building (often referred to as the "Gherkin," now a world-famous landmark); and both Renzo Piano's equally radical London Bridge Tower and KPF's Heron Tower in Bishopsgate have the green light for development.

Richard Rogers's vision of a city that is built on a human scale was pivotal to our vision for London's growth as we devised an urban planning system that focused on implementing quality as well as quantity, although we recognized that high-density must not always mean high-rise. We harnessed the skills of the best architects and planners in the world to design sustainable, comfortable, and appropriately dense development, and to commission and promote new public squares and parks to significantly improve the quality of urban living in our city as it continues to grow. We believe people of all income levels should be able to live close to open spaces and transport connections as well as the shops, services, and cultural attractions that make urban living exciting. We cannot afford to let our population spill out into rural areas and onto our precious open spaces where the only transport option will be to add more cars to our roads and more pollution to our city.

In recent years, a new imperative has emerged to take its place among these perennial challenges. As mayor, I made it a priority to ensure that London took a national and international lead in the effort to address the challenges of climate change. This work extends across almost every facet of our city's life, but nowhere is it more pressing than in the built environment. We set new standards for the environmental performance of buildings, pushing developers to achieve the greatest possible reductions in carbon dioxide emissions, and encouraged green roofs, sustainable cooling mechanisms, and well-designed green spaces.

London has begun successfully to redress decades of neglect and under-investment. Its self-confidence and vigor have returned, and it is experiencing record numbers of visitors. London will always be a city of some of the world's finest Georgian architecture, beautifully landscaped parks, and awe-inspiring river views. We relish our mixture of old and new, large and small, and the breadth of what it can offer to the world's investors, tourists, and the growing number of people who call London home. We must embrace change, and the opportunities and challenges it brings. Good architecture, design, and planning have never been more important.

# INTRODUCTION
## SAM LUBELL

TOP / Herzog & de Meuron, Tate Modern extension, Southwark // ABOVE / Olafur Eliasson and Kjetil Thorsen, 2007 Serpentine Gallery Pavilion, Hyde Park // RIGHT / Renzo Piano Building Workshop, Shard tower, London Bridge

**LONDON'S RECENT BUILDINGS** are some of the most vibrant in the world. From the daring shape-making of Norman Foster's 30 St. Mary Axe, more familiarly known as the Gherkin, to the cool, layered artistry of David Adjaye's Rivington Place, these projects are internationally admired and have played an important role in the city's conversion from an architectural backwater to a world capital of contemporary design.

Economic growth, resurgent popular interest in architecture and design, heightened political and nonprofit support and funding, and London's relatively new status as Europe's creative and financial melting pot have all contributed to this radical shift. Taking advantage of this climate, a group of talented firms are creating unique, artful projects that derive inspiration from contemporary forms and technologies, the city's glorious urban chaos, its fascinating collision of history and modernity, and its palpable energy. They range in scale from tightly-fit house additions to skyline-altering towers.

As recently as the 1980s and early 1990s, the architectural situation did not seem promising: government support was declining, development funds were low, and traditionalists were railing successfully against innovation. As architect Peter Barber confesses, "At cocktail parties, London architects were not proud to tell you what they did." But in the mid-1990s a perfect architectural storm began to brew. England's economy began to recover and then to thrive, spurring an unprecedented level of building and a phalanx of cranes to rise high above London's historic spires. Popular interest in, and acceptance of, innovative architecture reached new heights as sleekly designed consumer products gained cachet, as architecture began being covered in the mass media — bestowing celebrity status on architects — and as controversial buildings became popular conversation starters.

Not coincidentally, the government became more involved in the city's architectural future, involving architects in its decisions and utilizing design to help direct the city's economic fortunes. The National Lottery, created in 1993 during John Major's administration, has awarded billions of pounds toward arts, heritage, nonprofit, health, education, and sport buildings. Several buildings featured here—including Sarah Wigglesworth's Siobhan Davies Dance Studios, John McAslan's Roundhouse, Keith Williams's Unicorn Theatre, and Herzog & de Meuron's Laban Dance Centre—were funded by the program.

Such work has also played a major role in the British obsession with "regeneration," a code name for publicly supported projects that use striking architecture to draw people and businesses to neighborhoods on the model of Frank Gehry's Guggenheim Bilbao. Good examples are the formerly derelict London borough of Southwark and its adjoining borough, Lambeth. In the new millennium these municipalities have approved innovative projects like Herzog & de Meuron's Tate Modern (2000), Haworth Tompkins's Young Vic Theatre (2006), and Allies and Morrison's extensive renovation of the Royal Festival Hall (2007). The buildings have injected new life into the area, sent real estate values soaring, and drawn tourists in droves. Similar regeneration schemes are also being planned throughout the greater metropolitan area.

Under Prime Minister Tony Blair, in 1999, the government established the Commission for Architecture and the Built Environment (CABE) to counsel politicians and planners on architecture, urban design, and public space, and to institute high project standards. Mayor Ken Livingstone later created a similar group, Design for London, comprised of architects, planners, and academics. The group spurred London to call for detailed design review of proposed projects citywide, to enhance public spaces in the city, and to redevelop struggling neighborhoods. Livingstone and his administration also instituted the London Plan, conceived to augment the percentage of public housing in new residential buildings to 50 percent, contain urban sprawl, and promote an innovative sustainability policy called London CO2 that targets a 60 percent reduction of building emissions by 2025.

Several other architecture-focused groups and institutions have also been founded since this conscious effort to reinvigorate London's skyline began, testimony to the keen interest architecture continues to command in London. These include the Design Museum (1989), the Architecture Foundation (1991), and the London Architecture Biennale (now called the London Festival of Architecture, first held in 2004). Every year since 2000, the Serpentine Gallery in Hyde Park has erected a series of temporary galleries designed by some of the world's top architects, including Daniel Libeskind, Rem Koolhaas, Zaha Hadid, Toyo Ito, and Oscar Niemeyer. Meanwhile the British architectural press, one of the largest, has helped promote and criticize London architecture throughout the world.

The biggest beneficiaries from the early days of this renewed interest in architecture were the firms Foster + Partners and Richard Rogers Partnership (now Rogers Stirk Harbour + Partners), architectural giants that had been formed before the downturn. When they finally received a chance to build large-scale structures they took it, designing inventive buildings notable for their grand formal gestures and their exploitation of new computing and material technologies, enhancing the glass and steel high-tech style that they had first developed a generation before. In addition to the Gherkin, Foster's office also created futuristic landmarks inspired by simple but spectacular forms, like the egg-shaped, lopsided City Hall (2002), the skeletal Millennium Bridge (2000), and the swooping, parabolic Canary Wharf Underground station (1999). Rogers, who was awarded the Pritzker Prize in 2007, created highly visible structures like the Millennium Dome (1999) in Greenwich, a massive tensile canopy structure supported by a series of steel cables and spiky masts, and Lloyd's Register (2000), an office whose towering exposed glass and steel form utilized the "active facade" concept of its predecessor and set new standards for sustainability.

Many of these large firms' contemporaries and former associates have also achieved great success creating icons for the city's ambitious new architectural landscape. Alsop's Peckham Library (2000), an L-shaped building that cantilevers over its own courtyard, symbolizes regeneration in South London, while Allford Hall Monaghan Morris's Barking Library (2007), composed of two brightly-colored, rectangular apartment blocks placed over an inventively renovated library, represents ambitious redevelopment hopes for the eastern end of the city. Conversely, other architects such as David Chipperfield, Tony Fretton, and John Pawson employ a more austere aesthetic, creating projects of understated elegance.

Since the millennium, an entirely new architectural style has also begun to emerge that focuses heavily on immediate context. Its practitioners penetrate deep into the substance of the city itself for inspiration,

ABOVE / John Pawson, Sackler Crossing, Royal Botanic Gardens, Kew // RIGHT / Caruso St. John, Museum of Childhood, Bethnal Green

resulting in what the *Times* critic Tom Dyckhoff alternately calls "intellectual architecture" and "organic modernism." It celebrates the rich disorderliness of the city by incorporating existing or abstracted elements of the immediate neighborhood's unique characteristics.

Deborah Saunt, whose dramatic but contextual John Perry Children's Centre exemplifies precisely this style of architecture, calls the movement a "gift to the street." Sarah Wigglesworth's Siobhan Davies Dance Studios (2006) maintained much of the dilapidated interior of an old school annex while creating an arresting top-floor studio that curves and twists like the graceful dancers inside. Sanei Hopkins literally reflected the surrounding neighborhood of its Artist's Studio (2004) in shimmering mirrored surfaces and made the project's roof disappear with glass panels and beams. Architects such as Ash Sakula, Caruso St. John, Thomas Heatherwick, Henning Stummel, muf, and Witherford Watson Mann have developed strict forms of organic modernism with varying levels of literal adherence to context. Caruso St. John's renovation of the Bethnal Green Museum of Childhood (2006) meticulously maintains the feel of the original nineteenth-century building, almost invisibly enhancing it with improved lighting, an open sense of space, and subtle ornamentation inside and out.

Despite these many successes, London has several concerns to address, including a lack of ambitious large-scale work, a dearth of completed projects by top international firms, a convoluted planning process, and, regardless of efforts to the contrary, an often self-indulgent style. Yet innovation has not been deterred, and even more ambitious projects are anticipated in the near future. One example is the redevelopment behind King's Cross Station, master planned by Allies and Morrison. They are attempting to piece together a chaotic section of the city by creating new public squares, offices, residences, and retail space. Innovative ideas include using the area's gasholder triplet as a framework for apartments, former coal drops as shops and restaurants, and the old fish and coal yards as cultural facilities.

Elsewhere, to compete with the popular dockland business hub Canary Wharf, the City has initiated a handful of groundbreaking office towers that will transform London's skyline. These include KPF's Pinnacle, a tower composed of a series of sheared cones unfolding into tapered planes; Rafael Viñoly's 20 Fenchurch, a triple-glazed tower nick-named the Walkie Talkie for its top-heavy massing, and Rogers Stirk Harbour's Leadenhall Building, a colorful, wedge-shaped office tower. The borough has also commissioned major new mixed-use schemes, like Foreign Office Architects' Trinity, a £350 million project composed of three highly geometric glass "crystals," and Jean Nouvel's One New Change, a warped, undulating project near St. Paul's Cathedral.

The 2012 Olympics, planned to revitalize both the East End of London and the Lower Lea Valley, will be another showcase for London's architectural talent. Proceeds from the country's lottery funds have been redirected to the building effort, which will include a master plan by Allies and Morrison, a curvaceous aquatics center by Hadid, a stadium by HOK Sport whose flexible seating design will accommodate eighty thousand spectators during the games but can be reduced to twenty-five thousand seats after the event's end, and an Olympic Village whose design team includes many of the firms featured in this book, including Deborah Saunt David Hills, de Rijke Marsh Morgan, and Surface Architects, as well as international firms SHoP, Sauerbruch Hutton, and UNStudio.

Deteriorating economic conditions are beginning to slow new construction, and changes in city leadership may alter the pace of the rapid approvals for tall buildings and the highly ambitious social and sustain-ability initiatives that have become associated with London in recent years. Whatever political inclina-tions, economic fluctuations, or social trends it faces, however, the city is equipped to respond to them. Besides having one of the most unique urban fabrics in the world, what makes London architecturally unique is its ability to continually reshape itself, to adapt to changing times and circumstances, and to be inspired by its history without being burdened by it.

LEFT / Henning Stummel, Shouldham Street townhouse extension, Marylebone // BELOW / Allies and Morrison, urban regeneration plan, King's Cross

TOP LEFT / Heatherwick Studio, Boiler Suit, Guy's Hospital, Southwark // TOP RIGHT / Foreign Office Architects, Trinity project, the City // LEFT / KPF, Pinnacle Tower, the City // BELOW / HOK Sport, Olympic Stadium, Lower Lea Valley

**HERZOG**
**& DE MEURON**
LABAN
DANCE CENTRE
2003

**DESIGNED FOR A WELL-RESPECTED** dance academy, the Laban Dance Centre takes its cues from its neighborhood, Lewisham in southeast London, and draws inspiration from the abstract movement of dancers through space, a key interest of the academy's founder, Rudolf Laban. It also exemplifies Herzog & de Meuron's gift for dramatically manipulating light, views, forms, and materials.

The three-story structure sits behind a series of angular, landscaped mounds that serve equally well as a backdrop to outdoor dance performances or as a place to relax. The long building embraces its setting by curving gently inward, creating a subtle sense of movement and allowing its mirrored windows to reflect objects and scenes in multiple panes simultaneously, producing an animation-like effect. The facade also layers translucent polycarbonate panels of green, magenta, and yellow—colors often reflected on the surface of adjacent Deptford Creek—and achieves further depth and complexity through the use of a visible steel skeleton and concrete frame. This intricate and hypnotic integration of form and color was developed in conjunction with artist Michael Craig-Martin, who also collaborated with the firm on the light box at the Tate Modern.

studios
library
café
health

videos

A similar intricacy is achieved inside, where spaces are organized around a central concrete "road" that tilts upward from the entrance—fronted by a glass-clad library and training rooms—then snakes its way through the interior. The shiny, resin-coated floor reflects the dramatic elements around it: the angular light wells, black spiral staircases that mimic the appearance of volcanic rock, dramatically tapering hallways that frame the views at the ends of their lengths, and glass-enclosed courtyards that bring light and greenery deep into the building. Thirteen spacious dance studios receive abundant natural light that is colored as it passes through the multi-hued glazing, while a simple black, timber-clad three-hundred-seat theater at the building's center is the hidden heart of the facility.

citigroup

THE WORLD

# TONKIN LIU

## ROOF GARDEN APARTMENT

2007

UNAUTHORISED
OR ILLEGALLY
PARKED VEHICLES
WILL BE CLAMPED

**A FAMILY'S WISH TO REMAIN** in bustling South Shoreditch, a trendy section of London, while still being surrounded by light, air, and greenery culminated in this "green box," as Anna Liu calls it, atop a four-story Victorian-era warehouse. A flat steel armature secured to the warehouse roof via a large ring beam braces steel columns that in turn support the cross beams from which the two-story apartment hangs.

The apartment is entered via the first floor, which contains children's rooms—each with its own balcony entrance—and a colorful sunken "conversation pit" for watching television or socializing. Both the bright flashes of color and the intimacy of the bottom floor contrast with the open plan and pristine whiteness of the double-height second level, which offers dramatic vistas through floor-to-ceiling windows on its south and west elevations. Organized around a polycarbonate-clad central tower that encloses the bathroom, the second floor contains the master bedroom, which can be closed off via a sliding, carpeted wall; a study space; and the living room, which looks out over the quickly rising skyscrapers of the City, London's financial center.

Outside, the apartment's large steel balconies, clad with white steel-mesh grills, are planted with jasmine and wisteria, which provide shade and reflect the family's love of plants. The spiral staircase off the living room balcony leads to a timber-floored rooftop garden that affords panoramic views.

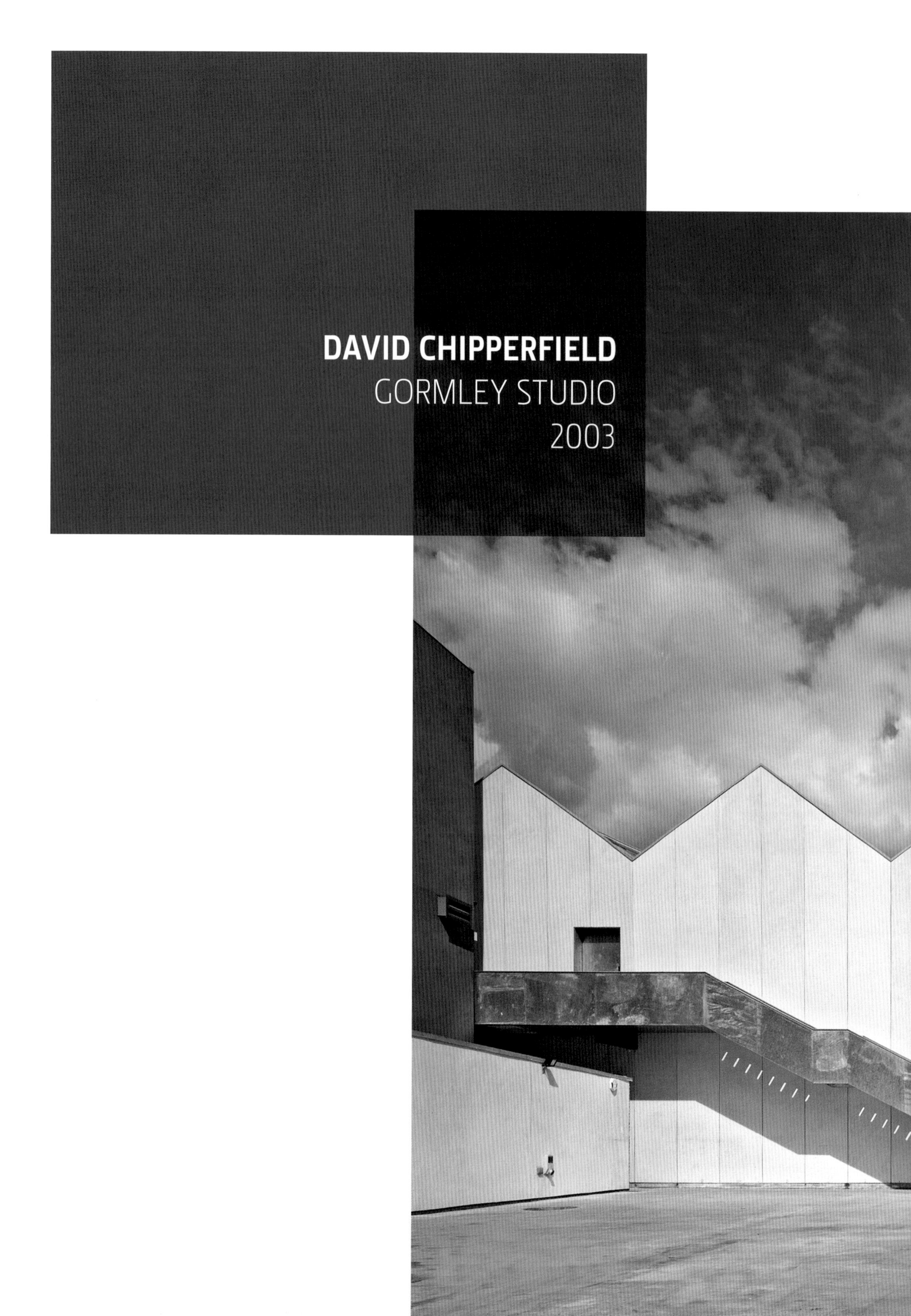

# DAVID CHIPPERFIELD
## GORMLEY STUDIO
## 2003

**ARTIST ANTONY GORMLEY'S** haunting steel sculptures, paintings, and photographs are among the most recognizable artworks in Britain. His new studio—just north of King's Cross Station and surrounded by industrial buildings—is, like his work, at the same time restrained and dramatic, pure and coarse.

Situated at the rear of a large paved courtyard, an area used to create, show, and transport works, the structure is coated with a serene off-white sand cement render and its facade perforated by only a few large square windows and large steel doors. The most noticeable element of this two-story steel-framed building is the rhythmic pattern of pitched roofs, reminiscent of nearby warehouses. Galvanized-steel stair rails abstractly echo the roofline, reference the artist's industrial crafting, and give the facade a formal symmetry.

Inside, the pitched roofs create cathedral-like ceilings, and soft natural light pours in through long skylights onto large-volume spaces designed for Gormley's complex, large-scale fabrications. The interior is divided into the main studio, a slightly smaller mechanical workshop, storage, offices, and smaller private work areas. Sculptures sit or hang throughout the studio, standing out against the stark white walls and simple palette of materials and shapes, and the overall effect is mesmerizing but calm.

**FOSTER + PARTNERS**
30 ST. MARY AXE
2004

PLA MARINE
PORT OF LONDON

**NO CONTEMPORARY BUILDING** in London is more iconic than 30 St. Mary Axe, or, as it has become known, the Gherkin. Built for insurance company Swiss Re, the glass, steel, and concrete building rises 590 feet above the dense fabric of the City, London's financial center. Its memorable shape—which can be described as resembling a pickle, a rocket, or an American football—has functions beyond the obvious one of making the building stand out. The slender top, which at its forty-first-story peak is a slim 65 feet in diameter, minimizes wind drag. The wider midsection—bulging to 183 feet at the seventeenth floor—allows for larger floor plates, which translates into more offices with views. The gentle tapering to a ground-level diameter of 160 feet accommodates a spacious, table-filled rear plaza that is pleasant and usually full of people, a notable departure from the more typical empty and windswept skyscraper plaza.

The rhythmic, intricate pattern on the captivating green-tinted and clear double-glazed reflective skin is formed by a series of diamond-shaped aluminum window frames and by the diagonal steel bracings that swirl along its height and manifest each level's slightly shifting floor plate. The diagonal bracings are in fact the load-bearing exoskeleton, and because each floor also radiates around the central service and circulation core, the floor plan is circular and column free. Balconied atria cut into each floor plate let more light into the center of the building, aid with ventilation, and serve as meeting spaces.

Energy consciousness and conservation guided much of the design. Several zones on each floor can be individually heated and cooled; electronic sensors control lighting; some windows may be opened and closed via sensor; and the diagrid structure minimized the use of steel in construction.

The double-height lobby, faced in a futuristic-looking corrugated, anodized aluminum, is fairly conventional. By contrast, the top-floor viewing deck, café, and event space is one of the most dramatic spaces in the city, its patterned glass and steel enclosure rising from floor to ceiling to provide exceptionally clear views.

**DAVID ADJAYE**

RIVINGTON PLACE

2007

RIVINGTON
STANDARD PLACE

ITY HOUSE
71
cargo

**WITH HIS NEWEST LONDON BUILDING,** David Adjaye has created a subtle and vibrant work of art. Located in ultrahip Shoreditch, the new home for the Institute of International Visual Arts and the photo agency Autograph ABP is the first permanent public space in the UK dedicated to minority-based visual arts groups. The deep, five-story structure, designed to match the industrial scale and character of many Shoreditch buildings, contains two large exhibition spaces for art shows, film screenings, and talks; a library; an education space; a café; offices; and archives.

As with his well-known Dirty House nearby, Adjaye clad the building in a heavy black concrete that gives it a sense of weight, refinement, and mystery. The arresting facade is a checkerboard of black aluminum panels and both flush and inset glazed windows that are placed at different heights on each floor. The windows become progressively smaller as they approach the roof, manipulating the sense of scale from the outside and providing varied views from the inside. Sawtooth skylights along the roof direct onlookers' gazes skyward.

The first floor's south-facing double-height exhibition space has a completely glazed frontage fashioned to catch the attention of passersby. The three-story atrium to the east contains a wrapping staircase, windows, and light boxes along its tall eastern wall that mirror the exterior's alternating pattern of light and dark. Deep windowsills extend aggressive shards of light inside, a powerful effect echoed in the self-lit balconies and sharply angled skylight shafts.

# JOHN MCASLAN + PARTNERS

## THE ROUNDHOUSE

2006

ROUNDHOUSE
DANCE
ART
CREATIVE PROJECTS FOR YOUNG PEOPLE
PRIVATE HIRE
Call 0870 389 1846 | www.roundhouse.org.uk
ROUNDHOUSE

**HAVING STARTED ITS LIFE** as a railway shed in 1846, this 71,000-square-foot performance venue in Camden is one of the most fascinating adaptive reuse projects in England. The round brick structure, shaped for trains to circle while being serviced, also saw use as a gin storehouse, and, starting in the 1960s, as a makeshift but very popular performance space where acts like Jimi Hendrix and The Doors played. But by the time the new millennium arrived it was clear that the drafty, out-of-date building needed work. Supported by Heritage Lottery funds on behalf of the Norman Trust, John McAslan + Partners updated and enlarged the venue while preserving its bones.

As part of the work, a street entry was excavated to the long-ignored basement, which had been used as an ash pit for the train engines. Within this space's arched brick hallways, modern glass-enclosed practice, media, and recording rooms were installed for the new Roundhouse Studios. Behind the glass, however, most of the basement's original brick walls were retained. Also in the basement, underneath the train turntable, the firm created an intimate, flexible, circular theater and socializing space called the Dorfman Hub, filling the space with contemporary furniture and capping it with a bright-red plasterboard ceiling.

The firm also updated the Roundhouse's highlight: its circular engine hall with an intricate wrought iron support system, which had become the main performance space. The slate roof was temporarily removed, and acoustic and thermal insulation on sensitive springs and a new steel web were laid down over the original wood rafters. The slate was then reapplied. The roof was updated with a ring of double-layered glass, called "the halo," and a central glazed opening, called "the lantern," which both illuminate the interior and help provide the necessary lighting and fly spaces. New balconies and much-needed facilities like restrooms and concessions were installed as part of the renovation.

A curved, three-story glass and exposed concrete addition radiates from the north side of the main venue and is connected to the main structure via a fritted-glass atrium bisected by steel beams. It contains a café, a small performance studio, offices, and support spaces.

Lift
Circle Bar

BELMONT MINI MARKET
NEWS · FOOD · WINES & SPIRITS
OPEN 7 DAYS A WEEK
NEWS & FOOD
OFF
SALES

BARKING
LEARNING
CENTRE
BARKING
CENTRAL

# ALLFORD HALL MONAGHAN MORRIS

BARKING
CENTRAL LIBRARY
2007

**THIS EAST END LIBRARY** is not for the faint of heart. Built for the borough of Barking and Dagenham, the brightly colored, unorthodox project includes the expansion and renovation of an existing midcentury library and the creation of two huge housing blocks above it. The work was part of an ambitious plan to remake and enliven most of the once-depressed area. The second phase of the Barking redevelopment plan will include the eventual construction of a new office tower, two more residential buildings, and a wooded square.

The two-story library was reclad with alternating glazed and insulated panels, creating a unique mosaic that permits, but still limits, natural light. Its facade is also marked by a projecting, rectangular conference room and by a stainless-steel entrance canopy. Inside the expanded and renovated library one finds an explosion of bright greens, blues, yellows, and pinks topped with a chessboardlike ceiling pattern of steel fins, acoustic panels, and radiant heat panels. Glass-walled double-height corridors to the north and south, which join the addition to the original building, provide additional space and light.

The six-story rectangular housing blocks perched side by side on top of the library, which contain two hundred apartments, are set on V-prop columns to lighten their mass. These columns form an arcade, floored with a checkerboard pattern of terrazzo and hung with gold-colored, hexagonal chandeliers designed by artist Tom Dixon. This space leads pedestrians from nearby Ripple Road, the area's main shopping district, to the new town square—designed by London firm muf—that fronts the library.

The buildings are clad along their street-facing facades with various textures of glowing resin fiberboard and with square aluminum balconies arranged in staggered patterns and colored bright yellow and lime green—a reference to the lemonade factory that once stood on the site. In contrast, facades along the inner courtyard are pure white, the severity of which is mediated by a pebbled area filled with floating green lily-pad shaped structures that are dramatically underlit at night. The apartment interiors are treated simply, with white walls and wood floors. Long corridors are somewhat overwhelming, but apartments are demarcated by bright signage and colors.

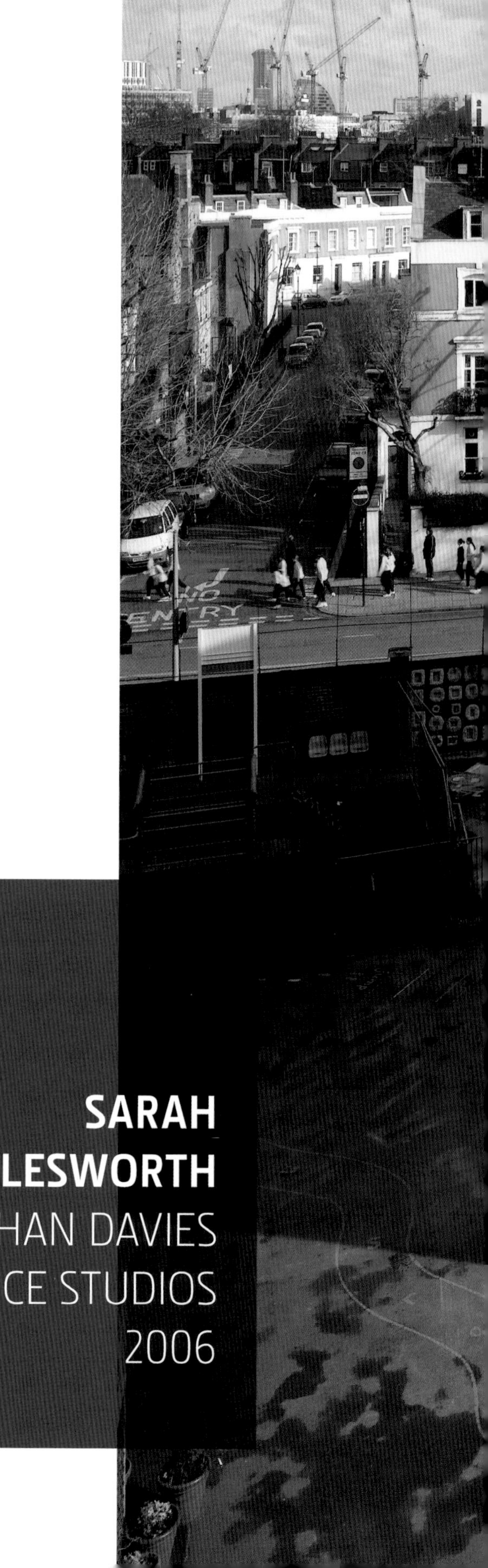

# SARAH WIGGLESWORTH

SIOBHAN DAVIES DANCE STUDIOS

2006

A D
1898

**THE STUDIOS FOR ONE** of Britain's leading independent dance companies, in the south London borough of Southwark, retain the coarse charm of the former 1890s school annex that is their home while transforming the building into a unique and memorable space for dance rehearsals and performances.

One of the most significant architectural moves was opening up the three-story building by unifying its once-cramped center with a double-height entry foyer. Here the architects decided to expose everything—old ceramic tiles, scratches, bumps, and uneven bricks—imparting an eclectic, shabby aesthetic that is continued in the new office area, lobby, small event space, and support facilities.

At the rear of the building the firm installed a hanging metallic staircase backed by a patchwork exterior wall composed of transparent, translucent, and tinted glass and louvered wood panels. Here, as throughout, the architect opened the space to abundant natural light while screening dancers from both the busy road that abuts the studios and from an adjacent elementary school. On the second floor the dance rehearsal spaces, a treatment room, and bathrooms were inserted into existing facilities, and a new hallway lounge for dancers overlooks the lobby.

The centerpiece is the main rehearsal and performance studio on the third floor, a huge glass-walled space highlighted by five ceiling "ribbons," as Wigglesworth calls them. These consist of overlapping and twisting steel beams, timber joists, and plywood boards alternating with curved translucent glass that permits limited amounts of light to enter the naturally ventilated space. This undulation is present as well in the billowing, blue-toned plastic roof that evokes the dancers' movements.

Call from here
BT payphones

# ALLIES AND MORRISON

ROYAL OBSERVATORY
REDEVELOPMENT
2007

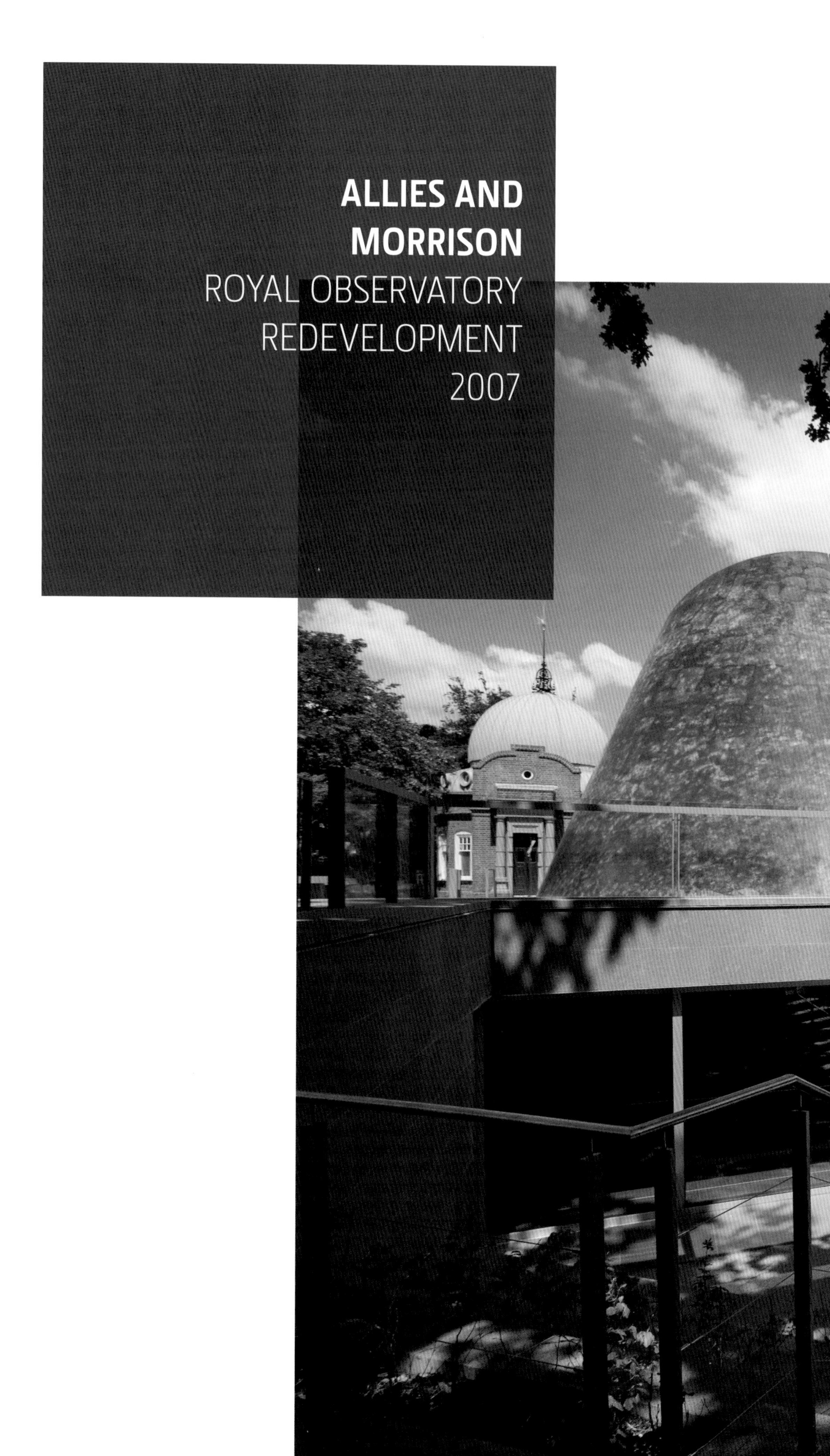

The Peter Harrison
Cafe
Shop
Toilets
Exit

**LOCATED JUST A FEW FEET** from Christopher Wren's Royal Observatory and from Greenwich's famous Meridian Line, the new Peter Harrison Planetarium, the Lloyd's Trust Learning Centre, and the Weller Astronomy Galleries were designed with both the landscape of the immediate area and the axes of the stars in mind. The projects are part of a renewal of the southern complex of the observatory that also included new landscaping and pathways to unify and beautify the area.

The single-story, 120-seat planetarium is clad in dark granite and sits directly under a slightly sloping, granite-paved courtyard that is the complex's unifying element. The building is accessed through a wide entranceway made of sliding and folding glass doors that open for events, allowing guests to spill into a new lower courtyard.

Inspires

The planetarium's dome juts dramatically up from the courtyard's center and is covered by a monumental slanted cone made of concrete and clad in an eight-millimeter-thick phosphor bronze carapace. The cone's unusual angle was created by aligning it with the axes of the celestial equator and the north star, a solution settled on after discussions with astronomers affiliated with the observatory. Its sharp change of height mediates the scale between the buildings on either side of it: the tall South Building and the much shorter Altazimuth Building. The bronze was hand patinated, giving it a textured look, and the cone's roof is made of mirrored glass that reflects beams of light from the sun throughout the day.

Just south of the planetarium the Victorian-style South Building, a former administration facility, was renovated and transformed into a space for the new learning center and astronomy galleries, featuring displays on the planets, the stars, and the history of the universe, among other things. The circulation was simplified and centralized by removing the central masonry core and installing a timber-floored, steel-clad helical staircase that creates dramatic contrasts between light and shadow. The firm also created new office and conference spaces above the exhibition rooms.

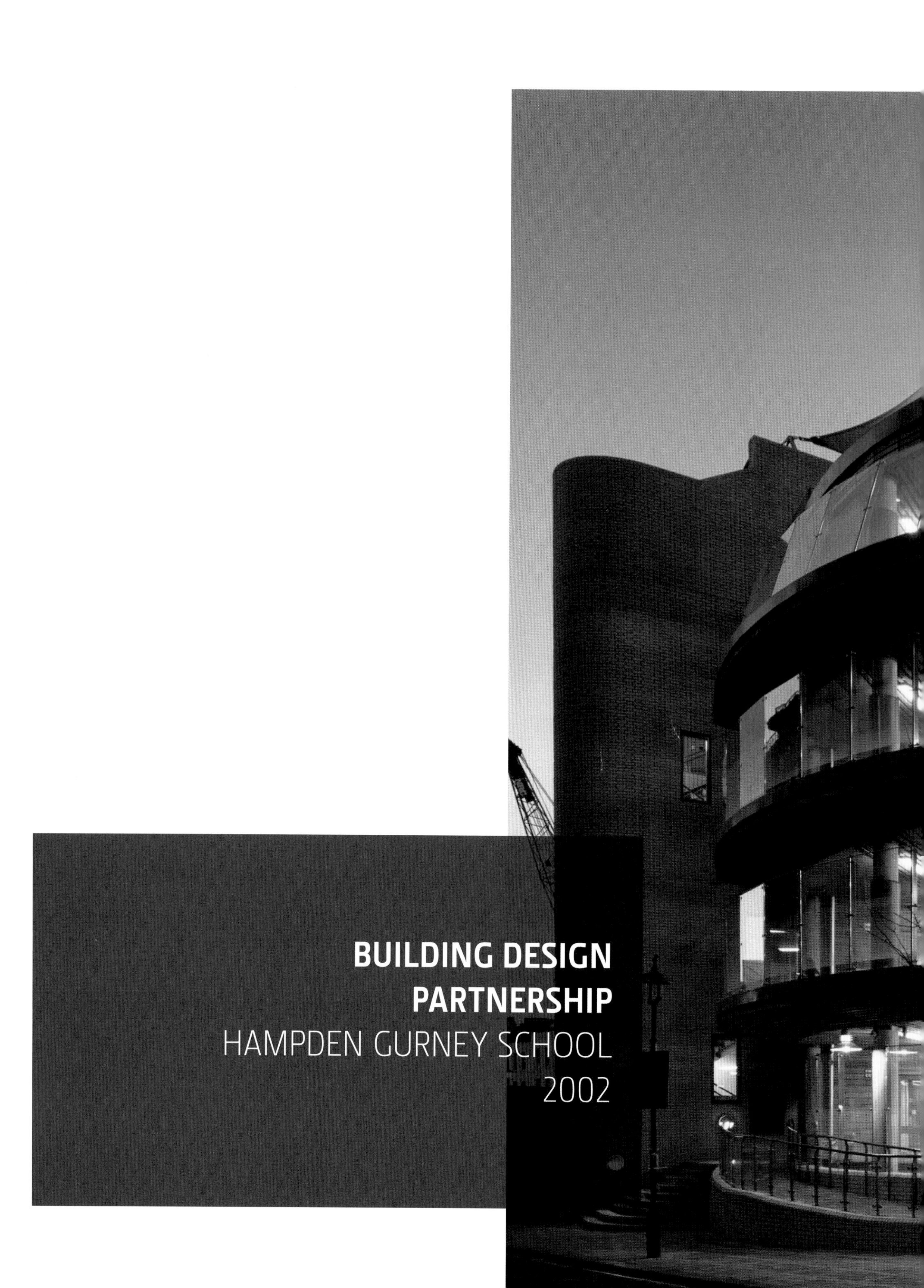

**BUILDING DESIGN PARTNERSHIP**
HAMPDEN GURNEY SCHOOL
2002

MAN
OLD ENGLISH GENTLEMA
FEE REPUBLIC
HOT
PANINI
COOL
£3.95

**THE 240-STUDENT** primary school, serving students ages three to eleven, is situated on a World War II bomb site a few blocks from the Marble Arch in central London. The steel-frame structure is a remarkably creative solution for a tight urban lot that once contained a very ordinary school and playground. Building Design Partnership redeveloped the site into a five-story, beehive-shaped facility and also designed a large private housing development around it—they overlook the same courtyard—that helps fund the school. Play decks surfaced with springy recycled rubber flooring jut out from the building's front, south-facing elevation at each level. They are partially enclosed by glass panels, thus allowing both natural ventilation and views of the neighborhood.

North-facing classrooms, distanced from street noise and harsh light, overlook the interior courtyard. They are separated from the play decks via cedar-clad enclosures that soften these elevations. Older age groups are located on higher floors, and students "grow up" the school, says architect Tony McGuirk. But all floors open up to a central atrium, which unifies the school and allows light to penetrate to the ground floor. A tentlike fabric structure at roof level covers the atrium and reinforces the school's iconic appearance. The large-scale arch under the sail-like covering extends downward to ground level, supporting the column-free atrium and open lower level, which contains a large congregation space.

Before completion of the new building, the school was 50 percent undersubscribed, McGuirk points out. Now it is 100 percent oversubscribed, and its success has led the firm to construct schools of similar design elsewhere in England.

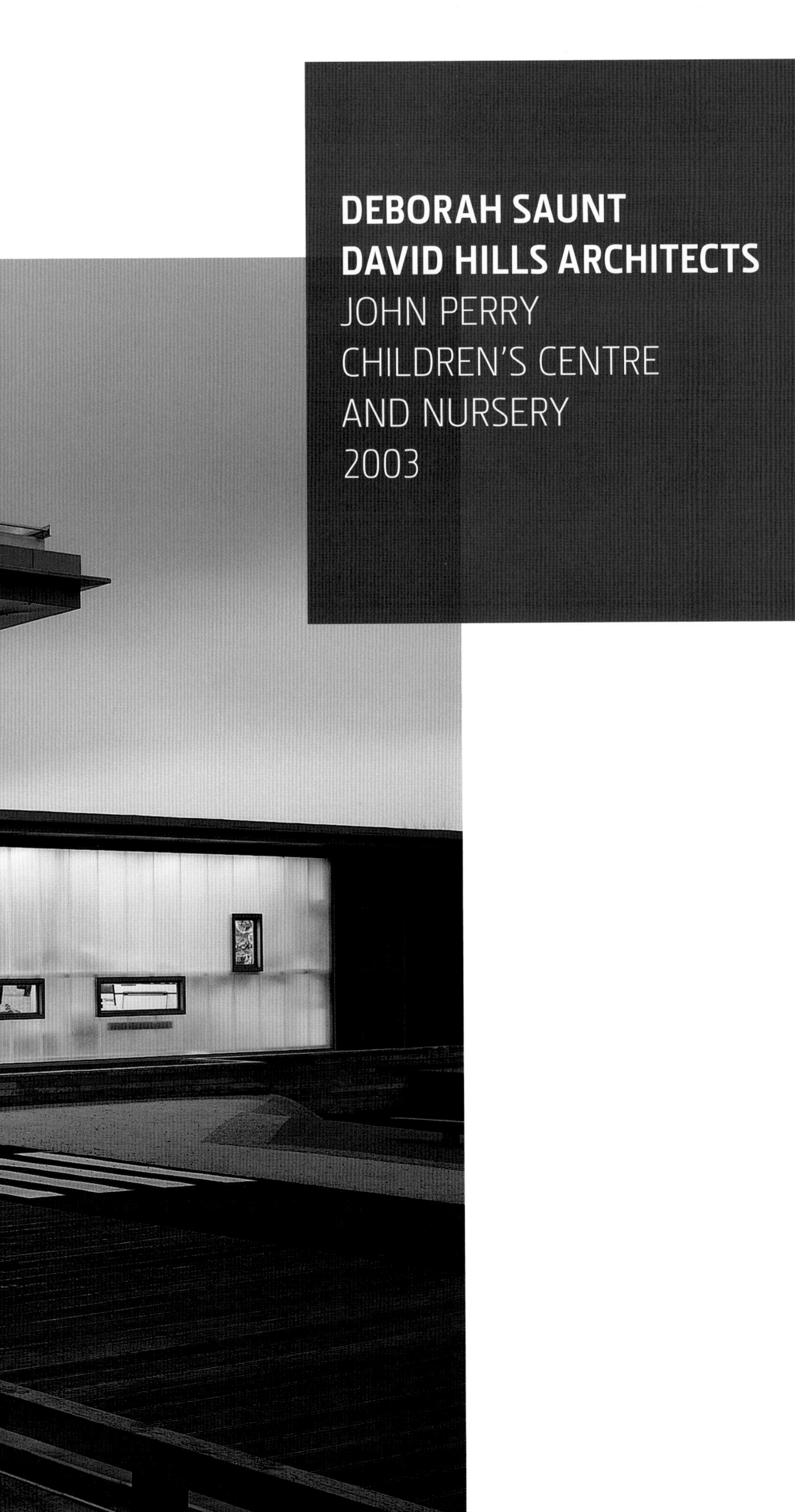

## DEBORAH SAUNT
## DAVID HILLS ARCHITECTS

JOHN PERRY
CHILDREN'S CENTRE
AND NURSERY
2003

**INTIMATE SCALE, INVENTIVE SPACE ARRANGEMENT,** innovative materials, and adventurous landscaping have helped shape inviting and exciting learning centers on the eastern edge of London. These long, single-story buildings by Deborah Saunt David Hills Architects are clad in a purplish silver Dutch brick—a material that references both traditional school design and Dagenham's industrial past—and in translucent corrugated polycarbonate, which allows light penetration while minimizing heat gain. The interior finishes are a warm, tactile combination of cork and oak. Classrooms are essentially one continuous space divided into distinct zones; clerestory windows between rooms connect the overall space and maximize light and ventilation.

Bold, hilly landscaping in the children's center and a series of layered activity zones in the nursery — including a beach, a water trough, and a climbing wall within the adjacent school's courtyard — promote outdoor learning by making it fun. The complex's main visual highlight is also located outside: a 26-foot-long canopy made of a grid of steel beams that shades and shelters the outdoor areas. Extending from the nursery school, the structure is cantilevered to keep children from bumping into columns, Saunt explains. Another unusual element is the mirrored sculpture at the intersection of the paths between the two facilities, designed by the architects to encourage parents to linger and converse. A similar sculpture was placed in the nursery school playground.

## ALISON BROOKS ARCHITECTS

WRAP HOUSE

2005

**THIS SINGLE-STORY** rear addition to an Edwardian house in Chiswick, west London, gets its name from its unique composition, in which a single surface appears to wrap around the back of the house and extend into the backyard. The project unfolds in a series of angular movements that articulate its internal and exterior spaces and guide the eye from one zone to the next.

Planks of ipê, a weather-resistant South American wood, line the roof and walls and extend seamlessly from the interior floor to the deck outside. The addition's form, says architect Rob Liedgens, evolved after intense experimentation with both computer and physical models. The shape that resulted takes full advantage of available space, captures natural light, and maximizes garden views.

A continuous skylight where the addition meets the main house enhances the airiness of the interior, as do vertical mirrors that hide the steel structure, and sliding glass doors that open to the outdoors. The architects achieved continuity by removing the original brick wall on the first floor, opening up a clear sight line from front door to garden. White interior walls create a serene atmosphere that meshes with the rest of the house.

The roof extends beyond the addition's envelope and out to the yard's side wall, creating a covered exterior space that further blurs the line between indoors and out. The structure sits on small piles that leave the ground basically untouched, reducing the disruption of the yard.

# AMIN TAHA ARCHITECTS

## GAZZANO HOUSE

## 2005

**MANY CONTEMPORARY BUILDINGS** aim to be light and transparent. But young London architect Amin Taha took the opposite route when designing the Gazzano House, a six-floor residential building on busy Farringdon Road in Clerkenwell. He focused instead on the solidity of forms and materials to give the project a striking robustness.

The concrete block–framed building is sided with reddish Cor-Ten steel panels, a rough material that fits well with the industrial scale and character of the area and that will change texture over time. Held in place via aluminum rails, the panels are arranged horizontally, and they overlap as they wrap around the building. In order to maintain the impression of a unified steel mass, Taha oriented windows horizontally and vertically in a seemingly random pattern that keeps the eye from perceiving distinct floors. The lack of balconies, the inset glazing, and the small size of the building's entry also serve this end.

The apartments have been converted from market-rate housing to student quarters and have been partitioned into smaller units in the process. Still, floor-to-ceiling windows, tall ceilings, and continuous white surfaces preserve a sense of space within a rather confined area.

HURFORD
FLAT
FOR S
020 725
for sale
felicity.j.
lord
251 9449
1 BED FLAT AVAILABLE
FOR SALE
Bairstow Eves
Countrywide
Clerkenwell & City 020 7490 1333
www.rightmove.co.uk
FOR SALE
020 7251 5666
TO LET
FRANK HARRIS
& COMPANY
020 7405 4444
www.frankharris.co.uk
LITTLE BAY

# ROGERS STIRK HARBOUR + PARTNERS

## LLOYD'S REGISTER 2000

Nº 67
EAST INDIA ARMS
BLACK SEA AND BALTIC HOUSE
65
mobile phone centre
... All these phones
mobile phone centre
REED
BENIHANA

**LOCATED IN THE CITY,** London's major business district, the 260,000-square-foot headquarters for Lloyd's Register, a risk management company, was designed to optimize light, space, and energy on a site that is almost impossibly constrained.

The fan-shaped plan, which tapers toward the front, was dictated by the angled streets, landmarked buildings, and large Fenchurch Street train station that enclose it. It is divided into "servant" and "served" spaces, architect Andy Young explains, referring to a theme popularized by Louis Kahn, who was a major influence on Richard Rogers. The tall servant spaces located to the north are the building's highly kinetic public face— fire escapes, wall-climber elevators, mechanical systems, and lobbies are all clearly visible through glass-and steel enclosures. This constant movement of people, elevators, and light can be glimpsed from the small, leafy courtyard below, a peaceful former churchyard protected from nearby streets by surrounding buildings.

Behind this frontage the complex is divided into five-, ten-, and thirteen-story buildings connected by two glass atria that draw light inside and help anchor, maximize, and organize the space. The buildings' thin profiles ensure that employees are as close as possible to natural light. Electronic sensors control the perforated aluminum shades that screen the long, double-glazed offices—sophisticated technology when the building was completed in 2000. So, too, were the heating and cooling systems, regulated by chilled beams installed directly into the exposed concrete structure of the dramatically vaulted ceilings. The dense thermal mass of the structure also insulates the building.

STORAGE

# **PETER BARBER ARCHITECTS**
# DONNYBROOK QUARTER 2005

PARNELL ROAD E3

**THIS PUBLIC HOUSING PROJECT** in London's East End is more an exercise in city making than in building making. Created for developer Circle 33 (now called Circle Anglia), the forty-eight-unit project was designed to "unlock the density of the site," Peter Barber explains. Its multi-story terraced townhouses — which each have their own entries and their own courtyards, either on ground level or on "notched terraces" above other units' rooftops — are arranged along a wide, paved pedestrian thoroughfare that becomes very active during peak hours. Neighbors' interactions can thus take place in a common outdoor space rather than in tight hallways and staircases.

Barber describes the style of the white stuccoed buildings as "souped-up minimalism," owing to their quirkiness and to their variously protruding, curving, or angular facades, windows, bays, terraces, and courtyards. Many of the units have similar forms, but a few take on unique characteristics. The "cheese unit," for example, is chamfered sharply to fit into a wedge-shaped site, and the "TV unit" is two and a half stories tall, with an exceptionally large window facing the street, maximizing natural light and, says Barber, giving the bordering public space a proper sense of enclosure. Inside, the architects were able to give the relatively small units a bigger feel by arranging small bedrooms along the length of large living rooms.

**STUDIO DANIEL LIBESKIND**

LONDON METROPOLITAN UNIVERSITY
GRADUATE CENTRE
2004

**THE ORION PROJECT** on the university's North London campus is modest, yet impressively complex. Motivating the design was the desire to draw attention to the university and its expanding graduate programs. Although the building is a relatively small 10,000 square feet, the architect's trademark geometries arrest the eye, thrusting themselves sharply up and down along steep angles and quite near to the adjacent Holloway Road. The northernmost section stands twice as tall as the rest of the building and faces the Holloway Road tube stop, announcing the building's presence. The concrete structure is covered with embossed triangular stainless-steel panels punctuated with large, angular windows framed in black steel.

The Graduate Centre is composed of three interconnected blocks that reflect the basic program elements of entrance lobby, event hall/lecture auditorium, and classroom spaces. It is also attached to, and shares some hallways with, a modernist classroom building located just behind it.

Inside, spaces are correspondingly askew and change scale and shape quickly. The main staircase to the second level tilts dizzyingly, and the ceilings intersect in lines that recall the constellations. Light gray concrete walls, dark gray window frames, and white plaster surfaces provide a neutral backdrop for dark red furniture, benches, and lecterns.

LONDON metropolitan university

# HAWORTH TOMPKINS
YOUNG VIC THEATRE
2006

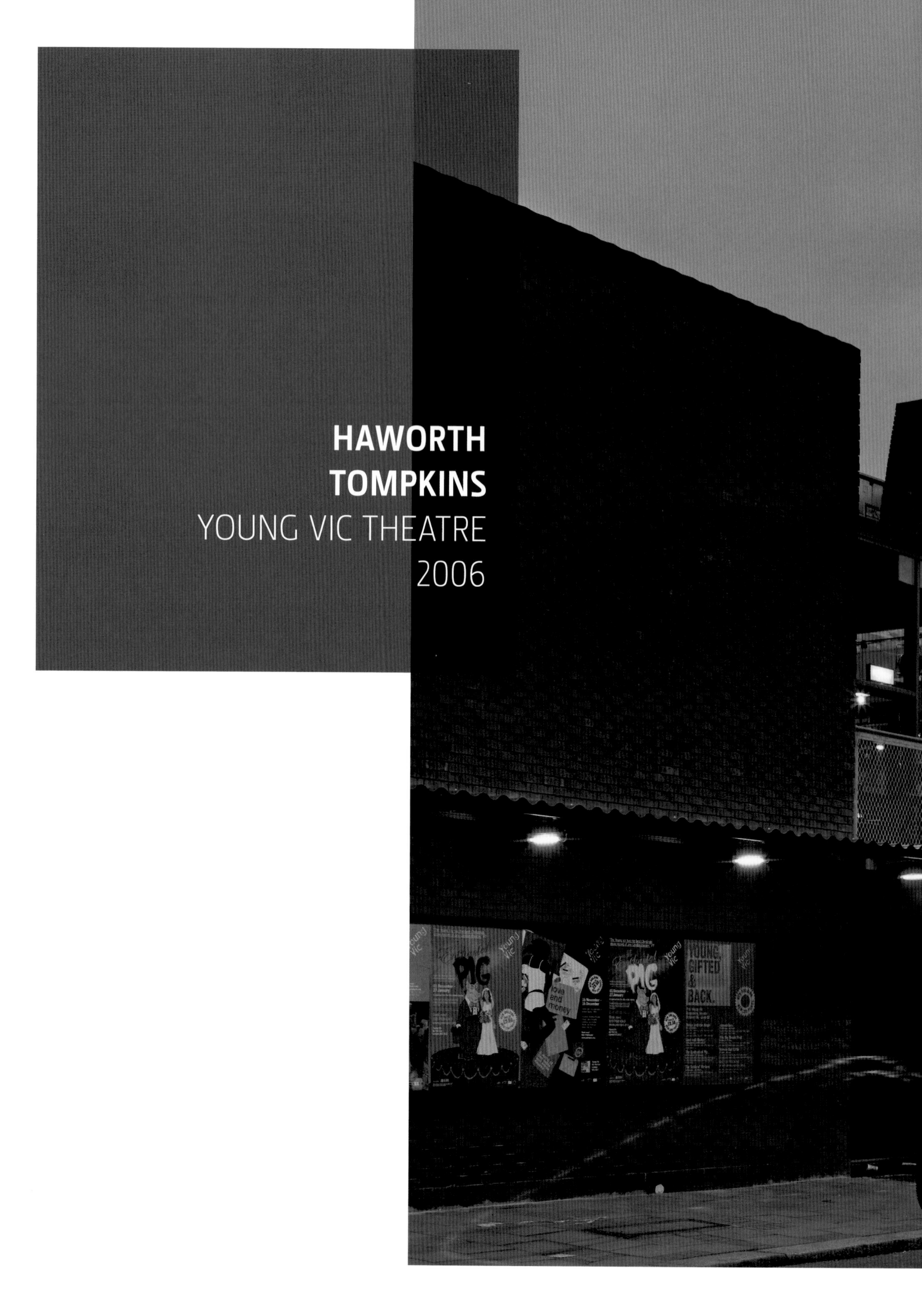

Young
Vic

**THE YOUNG VIC THEATRE** in Southwark, just south of the Thames, draws inspiration from its neighborhood's refreshing jumble of urban life, from the haphazard and often-unfinished nature of theater, and from disorder in general. This aesthetic suits the experimental venue, whose varied performance troupes sought a space with a fluid identity.

Developed on a World War II bomb site, the original theater, a 1960s brutalist design by Bill Howell, used an adjacent Victorian-era butcher shop as its foyer. The expansion and renovation builds on these very urban, anti-elitist beginnings by improving upon and enlarging the theater itself, renovating the butcher shop to serve as a ticket hall, and adding a large new foyer and a new studio theater. Steve Tompkins describes the eclectic composition of buildings as creating its own neighborhood.

Young
Vic
TOBIAS

The facade of the auditorium was wrapped in cement board, to which artist Clem Crosby hand applied bright cadmium yellow paint. Over this the architects affixed an expanded metal mesh that allows the color to peek out, achieving an ethereal effect when lit at night. The expanded and renovated theater also has a new steel frame over the crumbling masonry shell, new seats, and new back-of-house spaces.

Next to the auditorium and the ticket hall, a new foyer maintains a street presence through its large glass doors and glazed balcony. Awnings and a planted roof minimize heat gain, as does a convection heating and cooling system. West of the foyer is the new studio theater, clad with an intricate weave of dark, profiled brick that complements the metal mesh over the main stage building.

The heterogeneous mixture of materials in the theater — exposed brick and plywood walls, raw steel balconies, quilted mirrors, unfinished timber frames, and ceramic tiles — are "salvaged pieces of history," Tompkins says. And, adding to the project's one-of-a-kind quality, the theater's set-design staff created much of the furniture in the foyer and the updated offices.

I HOPKINS
ITECTS AND HUGHES
ER STUDIO
T'S STUDIO

**IN KENTISH TOWN,** in the north of the city, a derelict former mews warehouse and its new addition became a light-filled gallery, guest space, and spa for a London artist.

The mews building itself was transformed into a guest house—its decaying interior rehabilitated, its windows left unglazed, and its slate roof replaced. Architect Amir Sanei says that the secret to the addition—which sits at the back of the owner's quaint garden—was to make it disappear. Its pitched roof, which mimics the roofs of surrounding buildings, extends from that of the main structure, but its long panels of clear glass supported by glass beams render it transparent. Where the roof flattens to form a sheltering canopy, the architects reduced its visual impact by making both sides of the canopy's surface mirrored so it reflects both the garden and the surrounding neighborhood. Glass folding and sliding doors minimize the bulkiness of the structure needed to support the canopy, and bring the outside in.

At the entrance a mirrored cube contains a sauna, and behind this structure a curved mosaic-tile shell atop a steel frame holds a shower, a bath, and a steam room.

# NÍALL MCLAUGHLIN ARCHITECTS

## PEABODY TRUST HOUSING

## 2004

**SOMETIMES A SIMPLE SOLUTION** can produce stunning results. This low-cost housing development for the Peabody Trust (one of Britain's oldest housing associations) in Silvertown in southeast London, is a fine example. The three block-shaped buildings, containing twelve apartments, are faced with gray brick at street level and on their side and rear elevations. But along their front, south-facing elevations the structures are clad with aluminum panels wedged between panes of glass. Affixed to the aluminum are strips of 3M radiant light film, arranged in alternating bands, which reflect bright, saturated purples, aquas, greens, oranges, and reds. Níall McLaughlin calls the material (an excellent foil to the building's otherwise gray exterior) "disco film" because of its dancing surface, which shifts constantly as light changes and as onlookers' proximity and angle to the building changes. McLaughlin proudly refers to the effect as a sort of "elegant tackiness."

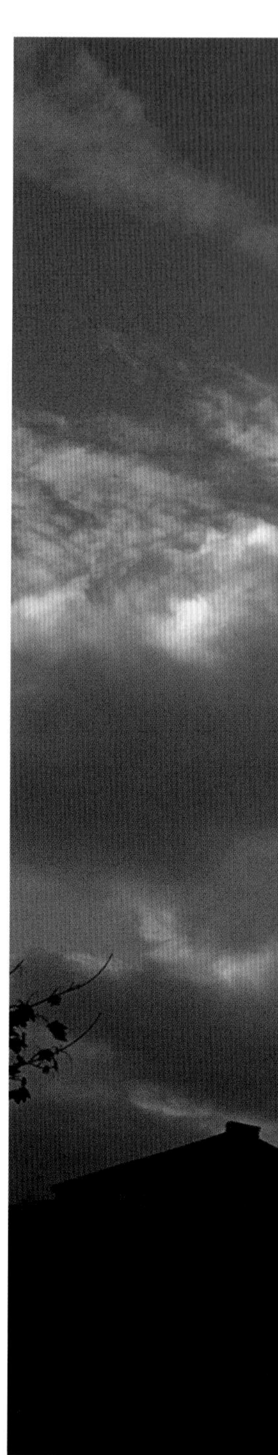

Simple white apartments each contain two bedrooms, a bathroom, a kitchen, and a large living room. All living spaces face south and open up at the corners with large windows to afford good views of the nearby Millennium Dome and Canary Wharf. Set back balconies separate building blocks and provide peaceful spots for lingering. Ground-level apartments have private gardens in back.

# MARKS BARFIELD

## LONDON EYE 2000

**OUTSIDE OF THE GHERKIN,** no structure built in London since the millennium is more recognizable than the 440-foot-tall London Eye, a reengineered Ferris wheel located south of the Thames just across from the Parliament buildings.

The Eye was originally proposed by London firm Marks Barfield for a competition, held by the Architecture Foundation and the *Sunday Times*, for a London monument to commemorate the millennium. While that competition had no winner, the firm decided to go forward with the project as its architect and developer. Despite some skeptics, they amassed support by heralding it as a celebration of the city through spectacular views—views that St. Paul's Cathedral, with its hundreds of steps, had monopolized.

The response has been more overwhelming that even the most enthusiastic backers of the plan anticipated. More than 3.5 million people a year have lined up to take thirty-minute "flights" on the Eye since its opening in 2000, making it the most popular attraction in the city. It has also, architect Julia Barfield explains, helped regenerate the entire south bank of the Thames. "People used to walk halfway across Westminster Bridge to take a picture of Parliament, then walk back. Certainly not anymore."

Steel cables radiate from the center of the wheel, a triangular truss structure supported on an A-frame steel hub that has two 165-foot legs. The frame is anchored via cables held in place with piles dug 80 feet into the ground. Amazingly, the entire wheel was tilted into place in just one day.

Thirty-two steel-framed glass passenger capsules are fixed along the outside of the 1,392-foot circumference of the latticed frame, providing unimpeded 360-degree views of the city stretching as far as Windsor Castle. Each capsule contains a motor that allows it to stay level as the wheel rotates. The double-curved glass of the capsules—aerodynamically shaped to reduce wind drag—was formed in special steel molds handmade in Italy.

# DE RIJKE MARSH MORGAN ARCHITECTS

KINGSDALE SCHOOL

2006

**AFTER ITS COMPLETION,** school officials quickly stopped fearing that this innovative Dulwich school would be a liability and started seeing it instead as a model for the British Building Schools for the Future program.

The 1,200-student facility was built around a rectangular 1950s glass and concrete school that Alex de Rijke describes as an example of "unfortunate modernism," because of its uninspiring facade, its unused courtyard, its extremely poor insulation, and its long hallways that led to a sense of claustrophobia, disconnection among students, and bullying.

To remedy the situation the architects constructed an inflatable ETFE roof over the courtyard, creating much-needed solar shading and insulation (regulated by adjusting the inflation levels), and setting the stage for a new 34,000-square-foot green-carpeted "public square" for the school. This grand hall provides space for dining, assembly, and social activities. It is highlighted by a new 314-seat geodesic auditorium constructed chiefly of birch and plywood. Thanks to the new open space—which connects all ends of the school—the firm was able to remove the enclosed hallways inside the old school, replacing them with large, open, renovated classrooms and airy balconies.

After the firm finished work on the main building, they proceeded to build simple but dynamic supplemental facilities. Both the sports hall and the adjacent music studios, which share an entrance, are distinguished by their twisted envelopes, their cross-laminated timber construction systems, and their metal siding. The sports hall is opened up to daylight with long clerestory windows, while the music studios are perforated with wild, fluid-geometrical openings and with double-glazed skylights that look out from the building like wide-open eyes.

# KEITH WILLIAMS ARCHITECTS

UNICORN THEATRE

2005

UNICORN

**LOCATED JUST SOUTH** of Norman Foster's City Hall building near London Bridge, this theater was built for a company that performs for children, from toddlers to teenagers. Yet its style is minimal, even austere, hardly what one would expect for a youth-related facility. The particular palette was chosen, architect Keith Williams says, because it would not "condescend to the audience" and because it was flexible enough to suit tastes that change rapidly through childhood.

A series of interlocking and protruding masses compose the exterior of the five-story building. To the west the main theater, wrapped in copper with irregular standing seams, cantilevers over the glazed foyer, almost appearing to float. A horizontal band of windows revealing the conference room also projects out from the theater, adding another layer. The foyer's glass curtain wall wraps around the building, fronting its west and south elevations. Above, a white stucco surface continues to roof level, while much of the rear elevation is clad in dark brick.
On the south face the glazed green room projects from the facade in a similar manner.

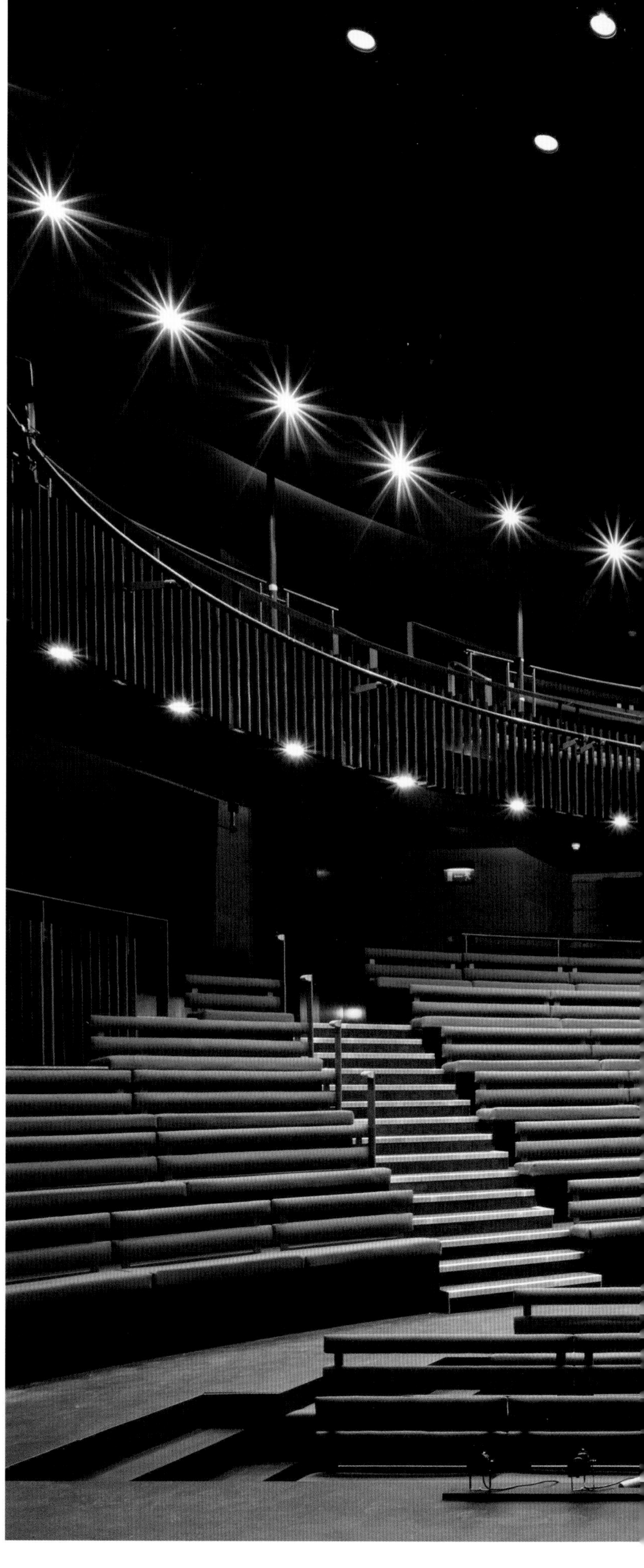

The interior of the double-height foyer contains an interesting combination of "rough" elements—exposed concrete ceiling joists and stacked, projecting concrete balconies—and "polished" elements—stone floors, pristine white walls, and walnut paneling along the tall, narrow stairway that leads to the main theater and the rooms beyond.

The 340-seat Weston Theatre contains a fairly steep, intimate arrangement of cushioned blue benches low enough for children that curve along a small balcony and around the front of the stage. A smaller, black box theater sits below. The facility as a whole has given this formerly peripatetic theater company much-needed back-of-house, loading, rehearsal, education, support, and office spaces.

# SMC ALSOP

PECKHAM LIBRARY
2000

LIBRARY

**SOUTH LONDON'S PECKHAM LIBRARY** displays Will Alsop's characteristic taste for the bizarre. But its strangest elements are also its most effective and what have helped make the library a centerpiece for regeneration in this economically depressed area.

Thin, angled columns support the L-shaped, four-story building as it cantilevers far over its own urban plaza. This formation creates what Alsop calls "an urban umbrella" where people naturally congregate. The space, which feels like a void in the building because its dark coloring contrasts with the irregular patinated green copper cladding on the facade, has become one of the area's central meeting points. The entrance is fairly unassuming, and its lower floors contain education and support spaces, as well as a borough office where local residents can send mail and pay bills. The library's centerpiece is its double-height main reading room located on the top floor, offering visitors spectacular views of their neighborhood from the front and of the central London skyline from the rear. Low-set windows looking south help readers sitting at desks keep this view almost to themselves. Three bulbous, timber-clad pods suspended on columns contain peaceful reading rooms, children's spaces, and classrooms. The pods puncture the ceiling, allowing natural light to pour into them and into the reading room below. A huge red steel "tongue" projecting from the top of the building screens the largest skylight, filtering the sun's rays.

In back the firm created a glass and steel curtain wall composed of a grid of clear, orange, red, and yellow glass. This facade is further activated by the visible movement of elevators and of people walking up and down stairs.

Fiction
Read this...!

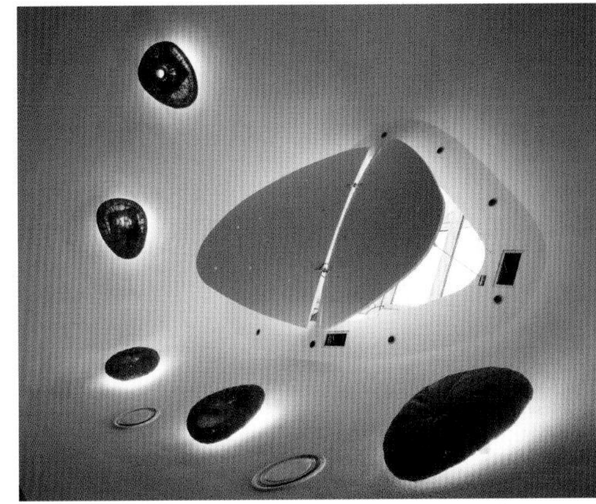

Languages
Fiction
Fiction

**BIRDS**
**PORTCHMOUTH**
**RUSSUM**

PLASHET SCHOOL
FOOTBRIDGE
2000

**THE 220-FOOT-LONG** Plashet School Footbridge, connecting the school's original 1930s building with a 1960s addition to the north, hovers high above a busy road in Newham, East London. The eye-catching bridge's core structure consists of a simple steel deck mounted on sculptural blue (the school's color) stiltlike steel piers. The deck rises up the sides, doubling as the balustrade, and is covered with lightweight and light-diffusing white Teflon fabric panels stretched over a series of galvanized-steel hoops. The hoops alternate directions, creating a unique, saddle-shaped profile that architect Michael Russum says students have likened to a caterpillar or a line of vertebrae. The design's steel-and-fabric composition and industrial scale evoke the area's famed shipyards.

The bridge curves around a large tree, then straightens again before entering the buildings on each side. At its halfway point a triangular folded-steel viewing gallery juts out over the street.

# FEATHERSTONE ASSOCIATES

SOUTH ESSEX RAPE AND INCEST CENTRE

2005

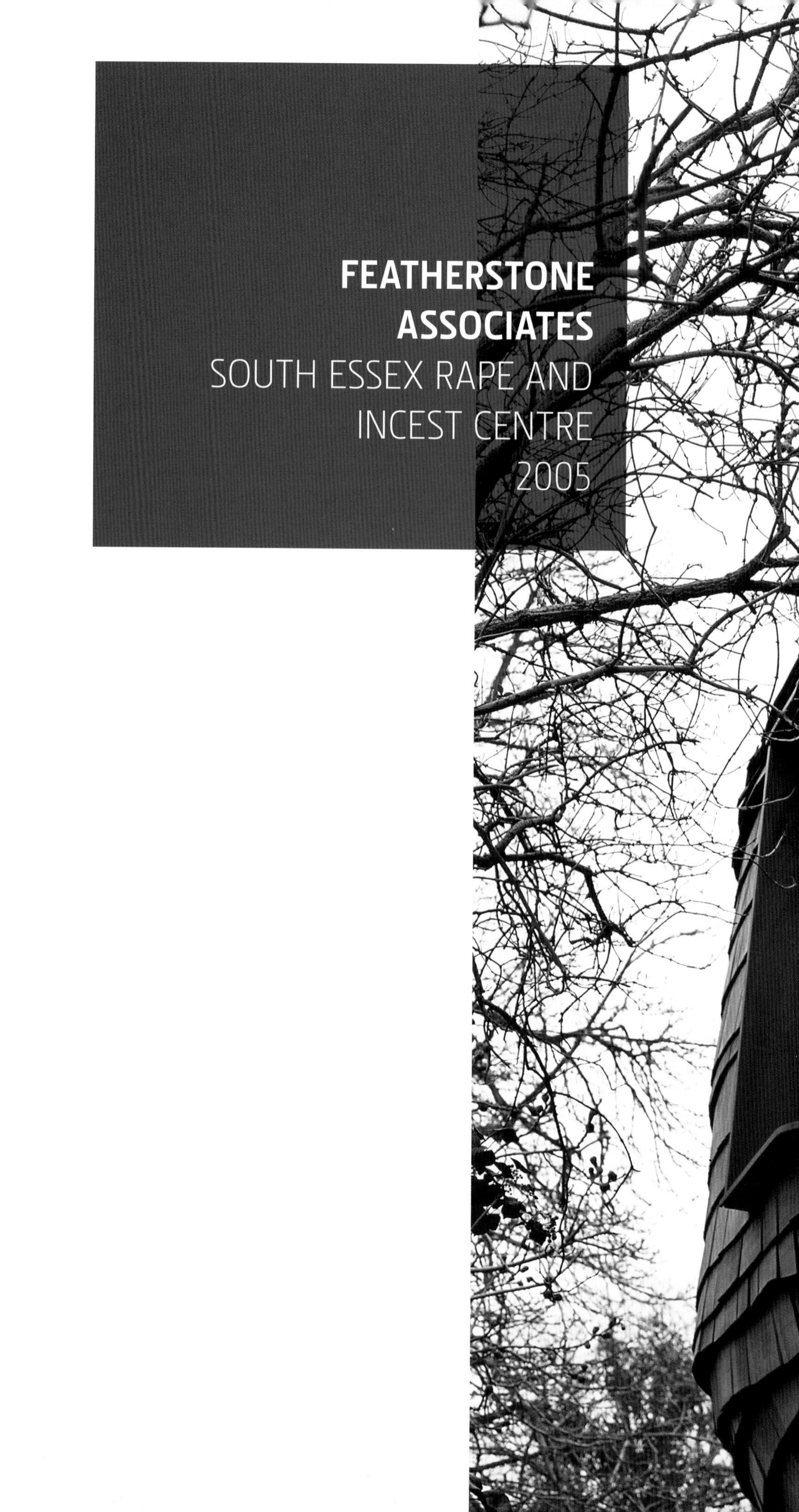

**FOR THE CHALLENGING TASK** of refurbishing and enlarging this center, housed in a bleak, institutional church hall just outside the eastern boundary of London, the firm's goal was not only to give it significantly more space and update its outdated facilities, but to help soothe visiting women and make them feel safe. The result is a very effective, well-organized facility that still provides a warm, sheltered escape.

The space is organized around a winding maroon-colored, cedar-clad "ribbon wall" that separates the main offices from the counseling rooms. Its shape carves out small nooks, and it provides privacy for women visiting the center, whereas previously women had to enter through the business offices.

The counseling rooms each have their own color scheme — yellow, orange, or green — and their large windows, which overlook a church graveyard, are partially covered with frosted glass for privacy. Outside two of the rooms are projecting podlike window bays that provide a small, comfortable area for repose and counseling. Inside, these "listening ears," as they are nicknamed, are cushioned with colored leather; outside, the bays are clad with timber shingles, an organic aesthetic that calls to mind a tree house.

The modern, white offices, which have been expanded by more than 50 percent, include a meeting room, a waiting area, and a south-facing balcony. Built-in storage also opens up what had been a cramped space.

# MAKE ARCHITECTS

55 BAKER STREET

2008

**THIS PROJECT IN LONDON'S** upscale Marylebone neighborhood is the most conspicuous structure yet by Make Architects, a practice formed in 2004 by Ken Shuttleworth, formerly of Foster + Partners. The firm transformed a 1950s office building—the aging former headquarters of Marks & Spencer—into a modern, iconic structure containing airy offices, inventive apartments, and dramatic public spaces.

Originally instructed simply to renovate this shuttered, modernist masonry building for new housing and retail, the architects took the request several steps further by completely altering the building's layout. Notably, three massive, cube-shaped sections of the structure were removed to create seven-story-tall public spaces. These voids were fronted with folding, origami-like glass infills, which the firm calls "masks," composed of diamond-shaped glazing within structural steel lattices. The masks flood the column-free public spaces with

light and help provide a connection to the city that was absent in the closed-off former incarnation. Offices wrap around the public spaces, allowing them to take advantage of the natural light and views. Angular glass and steel elements—fittings, columns, and futuristic lighting—contribute a contemporary aesthetic to what was a very dated building.

The ground floor of the building is clad with glazing and devoted to retail and restaurants, bringing new life to the formerly somber streetscape. The residential development was organized around a newly created courtyard, reinstating a row of mews housing destroyed during World War II. Twenty-three affordable private homes, clad in stack-bonded brick and topped by a sedum roof, were created within one three-story block in a modern interpretation of a classic London building type.

# SPACELAB UK

GREAT ORMOND STREET
HOSPITAL ORANGERY
2004

**ALTHOUGH ONLY A SMALL** component of the mid-twentieth-century hospital's larger redevelopment program, the project recently built into the heart of the facility constitutes a much-needed improvement.

Built on the roof of the hospital's central boiler room, the Orangery — a courtyard and enclosed seating pavilion — connect a new café also built by the firm and an existing cafeteria. Strips of zinc, medium-density fiberboard, oak, and ash that begin as decking for the courtyard continue under the tall glass doors of the steel-frame structure, curve up the rear wall, and break free of each other to project at various angles from the pavilion's roofline. The resulting gaps are glazed, letting in light and allowing views of the surrounding hospital buildings. The design adds what Andrew Budgen, an architect with the firm, describes as "playfulness, whimsy, and ethereality" to a formerly drab environment.

The building and courtyard have become very popular meeting points both during the day and at night, when blue fluorescent lighting placed under semiopaque glazed tiles creates a surreal glow.

# SURFACE ARCHITECTS
## LOCK-KEEPER'S COTTAGE
## 2005

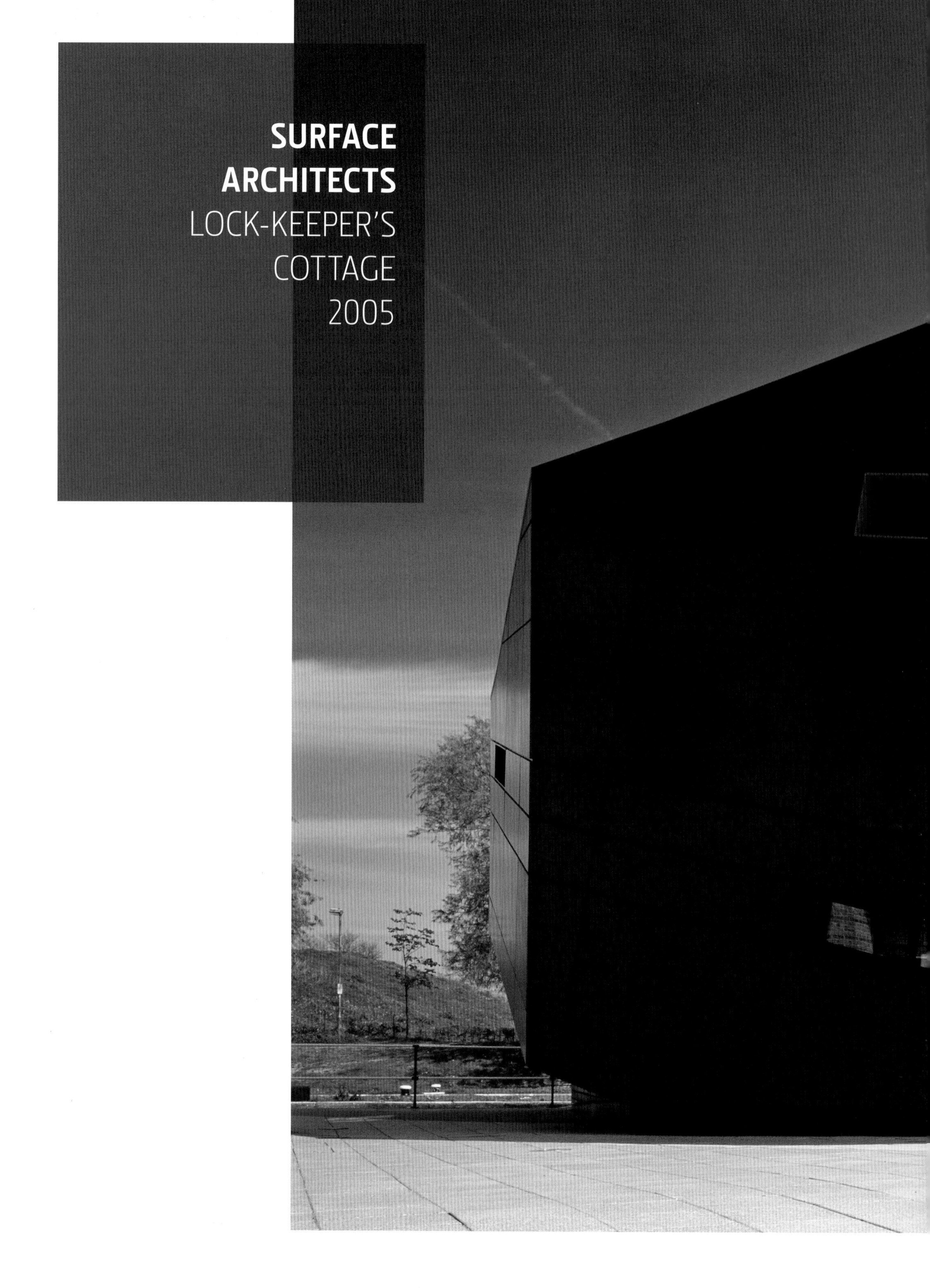

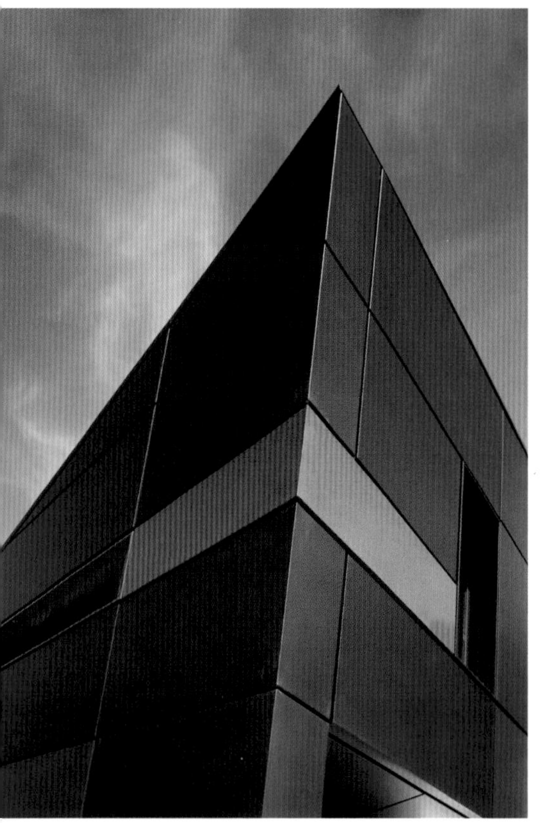

**THE LOCK-KEEPER'S COTTAGE** project on the Mile End campus at Queen Mary, University of London, in the East End is a small but significant addition to this quickly growing school. The addition to a nineteenth-century brick cottage along the Regent's Canal took shape on the site of a demolished pump house. It houses classrooms, study areas, and offices, and is just one component of an ambitious building program at the university that also includes innovative projects like Feilden Clegg Bradley's copper-clad Westfield Student Village.

The building's height and mass emulate the quaint cottage, but its form and facade—composed of interlocking shapes, angles, patterns, and colors—change radically as one walks around it. On the south and east facades a dark aluminum-panel skin angles upward toward the canal, like "a wing taking off from the campus," says firm associate Richard Scott, while a striated cedar section below this "wing" serves as an intermediary between old and new forms. On the north facade, a colorful, abstract composition made of rendered stucco and glass contrasts with the more austere elements of the building. The brightly colored linear art on this facade,

Scott says, is almost cartoonish and is a loose interpretation of form following function. A diagonal blue band mimics the staircase within, for instance, and simple geometries reflect the original cottage.

The large entryway, with its tall windows and brick walls gains space thanks to an oak bridge suspended above it. The second floor cantilevers over the canal, cementing the building's connection with the most peaceful feature of the campus and helping set the scene for the contemplative yet angular and dynamic spaces inside.

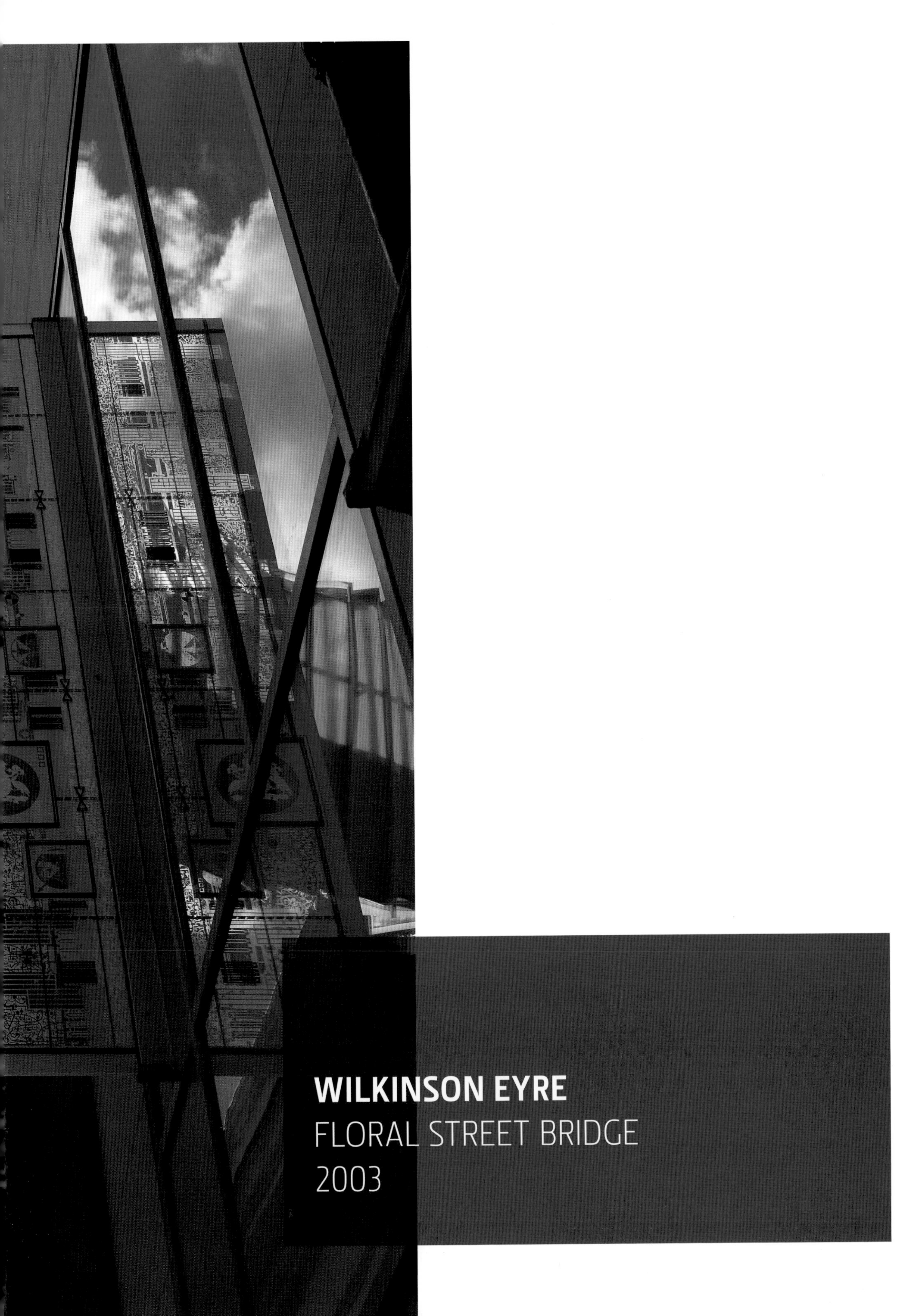

**WILKINSON EYRE**
FLORAL STREET BRIDGE
2003

ROBOT
WHITE LION
Paul Smith
CAMPER
BOOKS

**THIS MESMERIZING PEDESTRIAN CROSSING** spans high above a narrow side street to connect the Royal Ballet School with the Royal Opera House, near Covent Garden. Its twenty-three square steel portals, supported by an aluminum spine beam, each shift about 4 degrees. The bridge's level changes slightly as well, to accommodate the misalignment between the Opera and school landings.

The result is a curvaceous, sculptural form that viscerally evokes the graceful movements of dancers. "It comes alive," architect Jim Eyre says of the bridge's unique geometry. The alternation of clear and translucent glass between the portals gives the illusion of greater depth when the bridge is seen from street level. It also provides privacy for pupils who cross it and for the neighbors who live nearby.

The bridge gives the Royal Ballet School, which is tucked away from the excitement of the area, the dramatic presence it lacked, despite the recent construction of a new building. Embedded blue LED lights increase the bridge's profile at night.

# LOCATIONS OF FEATURED PROJECTS

Herzog & de Meuron
Laban Dance Centre
Creekside, SE8 3DZ

Tonkin Liu
Roof Garden Apartment
Shoreditch, EC28

David Chipperfield
Gormley Studio
King's Cross, N7

Foster + Partners
30 St. Mary Axe
The City, EC3A 8EP

David Adjaye
Rivington Place
Shoreditch, EC2A 3BA

John McAslan + Partners
The Roundhouse
Chalk Farm Road
Camden, NW1 8EH

Allford Hall Monaghan Morris
Barking Library
2 Town Square, Barking, IG11 7NB

Sarah Wigglesworth
Siobhan Davies Dance Studios
85 St. George's Road,
Elephant & Castle, SE1 6ER

Allies and Morrison
Royal Observatory Redevelopment
Park Row, Greenwich, SE10 9NF

Building Design Partnership
Hampden Gurney School
Harrowby Street, Marylebone, W1H 5HA

Deborah Saunt David Hills Architects
John Perry Children's Centre
Auriel Avenue, Dagenham, RM10 8BS

Alison Brooks Architects
Wrap House
Chiswick, London

Amin Taha Architects
Gazzano House
167 Farringdon Road
Clerkenwell, EC1R 3AL

Rogers Stirk Harbour + Partners
Lloyd's Register
71 Fenchurch Street, the City, EC3M 4BR

Peter Barber Architects
Donnybrook Quarter
Parnell and Old Ford Roads, Bow, E3 3DU

Studio Daniel Libeskind
London Metropolitan University
Graduate Centre
166 Holloway Road, Islington, N7 8DB

Haworth Tompkins
Young Vic Theatre
66 The Cut, Lambeth, SE1 8LZ

Sanei Hopkins Architects and
Hughes Meyer Studio
Artist's Studio
Kentish Town, London NW1

Níall McLaughlin Architects
Peabody Trust Housing
Evelyn Road, Silvertown, E16 1TU

Marks Barfield
London Eye
Jubilee Gardens, Waterloo, SE1 7PB

De Rijke Marsh Morgan Architects
Kingsdale School
Alleyn Park, Dulwich, SE21 8SQ

Keith Williams Architects
Unicorn Theatre
147 Tooley Street, Southwark, SE1 2HZ

SMC Alsop
Peckham Library
122 Peckham Hill Street
Peckham, SE15 5JR

Birds Portchmouth Russum
Plashet School Footbridge
Plashet Grove, East Ham, E6 1AD

Featherstone Associates
South Essex Rape and Incest Centre
The Hall, West Street, Grays, Essex
RM17 6LL

Make Architects
55 Baker Street
Marylebone, W1U 8EW

Spacelab UK
Great Ormond Street Hospital Orangery
Great Ormond Street, Bloomsbury,
WC1N 3JH

Surface Architects
Lock-keeper's Cottage
Queen Mary, University of London
Mile End Road, E1 4NS

Wilkinson Eyre
Floral Street Bridge
46 Floral Street
Covent Garden, WC2E 9DA

# ILLUSTRATION CREDITS

Numbers refer to page numbers.

© Hélène Binet // 84, 86, 87, 88, 89, 90, 132, 135, 136, 137, 157, 158, 159, 160–161
© Bitter Bredt Fotografie // 3, 121, 122, 123, 124, 125
© Tim Brotherton // 177, 178, 179, 181
© Richard Bryant/Arcaid // 7, 25, 26, 27, 28, 29, 31, 32, 33, 34, 35, 50–51, 54, 55, 57, 65, 66, 68, 69, 71, 126–127
Courtesy Caruso St. John // 13 right
Courtesy Roderick Coyne / SMC Alsop // 163, 164, 166, 167, 168, 169
© Tim Crocker // 16–17, 18, 19, 20–21, 22–23
Courtesy Alex de Rijke // 150–151, 152, 153, 154, 155
Courtesy Foster + Partners // 8
© Dennis Gilbert / National Maritime Museum // 74, 76 bottom, 77
© Dennis Gilbert // 108, 109
© Nick Guttridge // 98–99, 100, 101, 102, 103
Courtesy Heatherwick Studio // 14 top left
Courtesy Henning Stummel // 14 left
© Hufton + Crow // 52
© G. Jackson / Arcaid // 45
© Nick Kane // 139, 140, 141, 142, 143, 171, 172, 173, 174–175
© Katsuhisa Kida // 105, 107, 110, 111
© Make Architects // 182, 184, 185, 186, 187, 189
© Martine Hamilton Knight // 79, 80, 81, 82, 83
© Ben Luxmoore / Arcaid // 72–73, 75, 76 top
© Tim Mitchell/Arcaid // 10 middle
© Killian O'Sullivan // 194–195, 196, 197, 198, 199
© Chris Palma // 95 bottom
Courtesy John Pawson // 13 left
© Ed Reeve // 45, 46, 47, 48, 49
© Paul Riddle // 92–93, 94, 95 top, 96, 97
© Grant Smith/View // 106
© Jefferson Smith // 191, 192, 193
© Tim Soar // 62–63
© Philip Vile // 128, 129, 130, 131
© Morley von Sternberg / Arcaid // 47, 58–59, 60, 61
© Morley von Sternberg // 112, 114, 116, 117, 118–119
© Nick Wood // 144–145, 146, 147, 149, 200, 202, 203, 204, 205
Courtesy Nigel Young / Foster + Partners // 37, 38–39, 40, 41, 42–43